Who Stole the Fish?

Gerald Rose

CAMBRIDGE
UNIVERSITY PRESS

Dad looked into the fish pond.

"Where are all the fish?" he said.

Mum looked too. "There should be six,"
she said. "Now there are only two."

"Who's been stealing our fish?" said Gran.
She looked at the cat. "Was it you, Curly?"
"Me?" meowed Curly.

"Maybe the fish are hiding," thought Curly.
She looked under the leaves on the pond.
No, the fish weren't there.

4

Zonk! A slipper hit her on the head.
"Keep away from those fish!" shouted Gran.
It wasn't fair. Curly *had* to find out who
was stealing the fish.

She saw Dan sailing his boat on the pond.
Dan liked fishing too, didn't he? Maybe *he*
had caught the fish.

Curly went into the shed to look for Dan's
fishing-rod.

"He hasn't used that for a long time,"
thought Curly.

No, it wasn't Dan.

Vicky liked fishing in the pond too. Curly could see her net and jam jar. But there was no sign of any fish.

No, it wasn't Vicky.

Who *was* stealing the fish, then? Curly had
to find out.

That night, she hid in the bushes by
the pond.

What was that noise? It was . . . Bonzo!
Was Bonzo trying to catch the fish?

Curly crept up behind the dog.
"MEEEOW!" she yelled at the top of
her voice.

"AAARGH!" yelled Bonzo. He shot into the air. SPLASH! He landed right in the middle of the pond.

Bonzo *might* have been stealing the fish,
but Curly wasn't sure.

She waited.

What was *that* noise? It was . . . a fox!
Was the fox trying to catch the fish?

No, he was only looking for frogs.

What was *that* noise? It was . . . two rats!
Were *they* trying to catch the fish?
   No, they'd only come for a swim.

Curly waited. But she got so tired that she fell asleep! She slept until dawn. She did not hear a big bird flap over the roof-tops.

The big bird landed by the pond. Then Curly was wide awake!

The big bird stabbed the water with its beak. It caught a frog.

It stabbed the water again, and it caught
a fish – one of the last two fish!

Curly's fur stood up on end.

"MEEEOW!" she yelled at the top of
her voice.

The big bird flapped about in fright and
dropped the fish.

"MEEEOW!" yelled Curly again.

The bird was so frightened that it flew straight into the washing-line.

"MEEEOW!" yelled Curly yet again.

By now, everyone in the house was wide awake.

"It's a heron!" shouted Mum. "A heron
is stealing our fish!"

"Not any more," smiled Curly. "You won't see *that* bird again!"